from here
we build

from here we build

we build

queer youth write from their lives

FOREWORD BY V

(formerly Eve Ensler)

**EDITED BY SAM ROSE PREMINGER
AND THE FUTURE PERFECT PROJECT**

Celeste Lecesne - Artistic Director, The Future Perfect Project
Emma Jayne Seslowsky - Program Director, The Future Perfect Project
Sam Rose Preminger - Editor
Alex Alberto - Publishing Consultant & Guardian Angel
Lily Ariel Mueller - Youth Editor and Contributor
Rachel Ake - Cover Design
Alison Cnockaert - Book Design

Writer's Room Facilitators and Mentors: Alex Alberto, ALOK, B. Anderson, Truth Bachman, Beetle Bailey, Paras Bassuk, Lexie Bean, June Buck, Jacinta Bunnell, Matthew Burgess, Bennie Candie, Levi Chaplin-Loebell, Becca DeGregorio, Andrea Frierson, Alixa Garcia, Arti Gollapudi, Stephanie Hsu, Z Infante, Celeste Lecesne, L Morgan Lee, Sienna Liggins, Jimmy Maize, Jaycee McDonald, Junior Mintt, Sparrow Murray, Julie Novak, Reid Pope, Sam Rose Preminger, Toria Rainey, Cherie Rowe, Emma Jayne Seslowsky, Myles Tripp, Mia Arias Tsang, V (formerly Eve Ensler), Simon Ventura, Brandon Webster, and Sarah Jane Weill

The Future Perfect Project Team Members: Celeste Lecesne (Artistic Director), Ryan Amador (Executive Director), Kiko Wan (Director of Operations), Julie Novak (Producer & Program Director), Emma Jayne Seslowsky (Producer & Program Director) & Aliya Jamil (Graphic Design & Marketing Manager)

Writer's Room and the publication of *From Here We Build* is made possible by a generous grant from The Robert Gore Rifkind Foundation

"'Queer' not as being about who you're having sex with (that can be a dimension of it); but 'queer' as being about the self that is at odds with everything around it and that has to invent and create and find a place to speak and to thrive and to live." —bell hooks

thefutureperfectproject.org

In Loving Memory of Julie Novak

TABLE OF CONTENTS

FOREWORD

from V
(formerly Eve Ensler)

"Tell me everything and we will change for the better."

Judith Butler wrote, "we form ourselves in the vocabularies we did not choose, and sometimes we have to reject those vocabularies or actively develop new ones." *From Here We Build: Queer Youth Write From Their Lives* is the assertion of a new poetic vocabulary rising from the daily necessity of queer youth to find the words to describe the "I" that is always in motion, always evolving, always trying to assert itself through gender, sexuality, relationship and possibility. The feisty rebellious "I" determined to clear away all that has stifled, outlawed and punished it. The "I," as poet Lily Ariel Mueller wrote, is "forever coming of age."

This volume could have been called Queer Youth Write **for** their Lives, or Write **into** their Lives or Write **out of** their lives. The almost obsessive seeking of the most authentic version of self is the engine churning through this slim, powerful volume. As Seoyeon Park's spellbinding poem, "*You Must*," directs us:

"you have to trust **you have to you have to you have to.**

you will eat yourself alive if you don't."

And yet these poems are ironic, vulnerable, sometimes sad, often aching in the impossibility of ever arriving at a static place of self. These poets are brave gender explorers cast out in a non-binary galaxy, willing to be lost, willing to sacrifice safety for discovery, acceptance for becoming. As Ari Ochoa-Petzold writes, "You ended up falling for the whole world, not because gender isn't a wall for love, but because you know yourself so deeply that other people aren't strangers to you."

The book is a collective reclamation, a sourcing of a new language discovering itself in the queer present which is always simultaneously an imagined future. These poets, these poems won't be put in a box. No. "They are casting away the borderlands stitched on their bodies." They are writing a generation into existence.

Indeed. As Lily Mueller writes, "This will be a home for everyone yet-to-come and for every bygone soul. I care so much. Tell me everything and we will change for the better."

V (formerly Eve Ensler)
(she/her)

PREFACE

*from Celeste Lecesne, Artistic Director
of The Future Perfect Project*

This anthology features original writing by the young people of
The Future Perfect Project (FPP), a national arts initiative dedi-
cated to amplifying the voices of LGBTQIA+ youth. Since 2020,
FPP has been hosting **Writer's Room**, a free, online workshop that
focuses on developing writing skills for LGBTQIA+ creatives of
all skill levels, ages 13-19. We gather regularly to discuss topics
through a queer lens, respond to writing prompts, and honor the
writer in all of us. All the work you are about to read was created
between 2020 and 2024, and each poem is followed by a writing
prompt that either inspired the written work or was inspired by
the work itself. The point of this collection is to celebrate the cour-
age and creativity of young queer writers who are just beginning
to develop their creative voices and also to inspire those who want
to expand and develop an already existing writing practice.

The Writer's Room workshop is open to anyone who wants to
connect, share, reflect and respond with the written word. Each

session is facilitated by two LGBTQIA+ artists who are there to hold space, support a practice of writing and affirm an ever-evolving queer perspective.

Each season we choose a theme or a topic. For instance, in the Fall of 2023 we chose to focus on various aspects of the self: mind, body, heart, intuition, power and spirit. We wanted to know how these aspects of the self were informing the way queer, young people navigated the wider world. We invited Simon Ventura to lead us in an exploration of the queer young mind. Simon had recently aged out of our Writer's Room program, and he was enrolled in college as a psychology major. He mentioned that he was drawn to the study of psychology because he'd spent so much of his young life believing that he was mentally ill.

"Growing up," he told us, "I would look at other girls and wonder, 'Why can't I be like them? What's wrong with me?' At the time, if you'd asked me, I probably would've said that I had some sort of mental illness, because I was unable to act like a girl when I was supposed to be one. It was only when I learned what transgender meant that I realized I was a boy. I wasn't mentally ill. I was trans!"

Developing a self is a mighty undertaking for everyone, but for a queer young person, a reset is often required once they come to acknowledge and accept that queerness is central to their concept of self. As Ari Ochoa Petzold, one of the young writers in this anthology, told us: "What happens when you think that the holiness of your brain is instead an illness?" It's only when we begin to trust what we know about ourselves, what we've always known—our (w)holiness—that we begin to understand queerness not as a form of crazy, but as an essential aspect of who we are and who we are becoming. Simon's poem ("From Here I Build"), which he created in the Writer's Room workshop, inspired the title of this anthology. We felt that it perfectly expressed the attitude many queer young people have as they continue to develop themselves from the inside out. *From Here We Build* offers a new perspective, one that allows us to create a sense of safety, belonging and self with the language we have at hand.

We hope that the work of these young writers will inspire you to reach for the artist in yourself and encourage you to express yourself in whatever way is appropriate to you. From here we build...

...with love,

Celeste Lecesne
(they/them)

Letter from Youth Editor, Lily Ariel Mueller

The Future Perfect Project has been the greatest gift of my life.

I grew up in a small, rural area with no LGBTQIA+ representation or support available. Like many, I had a complex home life. I'd lived with unrecognized disabilities and mental illnesses since early childhood, and I'd known, since the moment I was conscious, that I was queer.

I stumbled across The Future Perfect Project (FPP) at 16 and immediately felt at home in a way I never had before. I became a regular at their online writing workshop, and participated in their performance intensives, their portfolio development program, and eventually, became part of the production team of their podcast, *I'm Feeling Queer Today!* FPP's programming has given me an invaluable range of technical skills, all completely free of charge, and from the comfort of my home - but more importantly, it has saved, and continues to change, my life.

I was reacquainted with play, joy, and wonder; I regained my conviction in who I was. I learned to be at peace with myself. For the first time in my life, I was shown the possibility of my own goodness: that maybe, I was wanted. That maybe, I was loved. That maybe, I did have a story to tell; something good to give the world. I was shown that a life of kindness and care was possible for me - I was given the gift of a future. I found the community I had always craved, a kind of family; met people that are so dear to me. Thanks to FPP, I had the confidence to pursue a higher education in creative writing, film, and theatre, and now have the privilege of creating art with my queer, trans, disabled peers - my people.

In the summer of 2024, more than four years after I first encountered FPP, I got to travel to Provincetown with members of the podcast team to hear from some of the young people living there. We handed them the mic and let them share what it was like to be a young person, often on the fringes of where they live. I could show them the possibility that they had important stories to tell. And that people were listening.

My dream since childhood has always been to help people, and people like me. I was a little queer kid who couldn't see a life before me - and I was given the chance to connect with kids who might be in the same place. My hope is for a future generation of queer youth to know their own goodness and the importance of telling their stories.

Lily Ariel Mueller (they/she/he)

from here
we build

VERONICA BUTLER

(she/her)

Lexington, KY

I Am an Imaginal Cell

I am an imaginal cell,
a tiny magic particle,
a holographic hope,
an iridescent fiber
in the muscle change.

I am an imaginal cell,
immune and impenetrable,
unmoved and undaunted,
endless and unwavering
in the face of the structured
stiff and terrified.

I am an imaginal cell,
dreaming, joining and transforming,
not afraid to forgive,
to love,
to spread my wings
and fly.

Imaginal cells are dormant cells in butterflies that are responsible for metamorphosis. When the transformation begins, the cells become active and work to restructure the larvae into a butterfly from the inside out.

Prompt: Shapeshifting is a special talent that queer people have. We often find ourselves blending into the background to survive, toning down our is-ness to pass, or flaming as a signal that we are unafraid. We can learn a lot about adaptation from our non-human siblings. Transform yourself into an animal, an insect, a flower, a tree or a bird and tell us what you know about the world.

That Girl

I envy her,

that girl I was 4 hours ago,
barefoot in the kitchen—
sweatpants, messy hair,
last night's Pad Thai.

Now I count ceiling tiles
with Maybelline eyes
in my sister's borrowed blouse
and shoes that pinch my toes.

I miss the kitchen.
I miss my Pad Thai.

Prompt: Every one of us, at every age, is a work in progress. We are never done with the business of liberating ourselves from false notions, old habits and limiting ideas. Make a demand or write a poem, letter, or song to the part of you that is not yet free.

VIRGIL BEATY

(they/them)

Philadelphia, PA

Fiercely Feminine

The beauty is there
Staring in the mirror, danger and mischief alight in topaz
    brown eyes
Petals fall, hesitance gracing the moment

The scent of fragrant peonies fills the air
The hem of her dress flows in the wind like leaves in early fall

The world isn't ready for her, she's beautiful and cunning
Her earrings dangle like suncatchers
She's poised and sure of herself as she strolls down the street

Her voice is light and feathery, yet animated and full of life
A smile graces her features, lighting up the room
Akin to soft, warm sunlight

Rose petals litter her path with each step she takes
Suddenly, her dress is swapped for shorts and a tank top

Deep and pondering breaths take place before candlelight is
    blown out
And in its place, a kingdom of feather-light beauty built atop
    the pillars of femininity

*Prompt: Do you believe your identity is forever locked into place, or is it
some thing more complicated and fluid? Write about the way you express
yourself as a queer person, whether that expression stays the same or
transforms from moment to moment. Does your queerness change in rela-
tion to the world around you? As the poet ALOK once said, "Look at the
seasons darling...Look at the sun, darling, everything else is moving but
you. So am I the issue or is your stagnancy the issue?"*

Like a Phoenix

You're gonna die
No no no not DIE
You'll hang yourself at the gallows of fitting in
You have to be you, dearest
Stop hiding behind social conformity
You're going to die

You're going to be heartbroken
She breaks your heart in the end
But it's worth it
You learned so much from her
How lucky are you to have loved
You are so selfless, my hatchling
And she broke your heart
You refuse the berries and water
The mirror becoming your worst enemy
You count the ribs on your body
Hoping to become a slender shell of yourself

Rise from the ashes, Phoenix
You are needed for greater things
Come share your rebirth with the world
For you are you
Rise up and face the world

You're going to fly, dearheart
You are going to see above the trees
And view the world for what it is
And it's going to be amazing
You will achieve many things
And it will be wonderful
My dear, you're going to fly

You will hurt
Soul crushing bone deep hurt
You won't be able to stop it
It'll seep into your bones until they ache
You'll feel like your wings have been clipped off
You will hurt

Your pain is fleeting
A temporary moment in time
You mustn't fret or dwell
Allow relief to flood your body, dear Phoenix
You will die again

It was all one nightmare
Dying and being reborn
Figuring out just who you are
What you're doing
But you'll get through it

You're ever changing and resilient
All you need to do is wake up

You're going to dream, baby bird
And when you dream
You will ignite
And your fire will burn

Prompt: Can you think of an example from your life when maybe you didn't have the words to describe something that was happening to you? Like a crush, or maybe something about your gender or sexuality— something you intuited about your queer self before you knew what to call it? Tune into YOUR dark place of possibility and listen closely for a prophecy of a possible future, either for yourself or for the world. Abandon conscious reasoning. What do you know?

HELIX CARPENTER
(it/ they/ she)
Farmington, CT

a manifesto in an epistle

"You have nothing to lose but your chains"—Karl Marx

Hey, you thieves,
You once thought
You owned me.
Maybe you did,
But that was rare.
My body is mine,
Mine alone,
And hell
Is it beautiful.

You may tell me
I'm wrong,
That the little indents and curves
Formed by my smiles and silly faces
Make me worthy of hate.
That the way my stomach bulges
Is an embarrassment.

You've turned my journey hard,
I'll give you that,
But I have made it.
You won't steal my happy ending.

The temple you have raided
For these three muddy years
I now steadfastly control.
This temple lets me cry,
Lets me accept
My stargazing brain and
My humor and
My love
And appreciation for uncommon topics, the invisible
Lines between countries, Wikipedia's 11.5 Calibri font,
The soundtracks of niche video games—

This temple lets me admire the ways I've gone,
The distance I've traveled.
So much so that I don't regret anymore.
You won't take more from me.
You may throw my past in my face,
And I may be uncomfortable,
But I don't retch at that thought.
I made my mistakes.

Mistakes are the human way,
And I make mine up a thousandfold.

So yes, I love myself,
I love my body.
So yes, I dislike my past,
But I won't disown it.
So yes, I still hurt,
But not because of you.
So yes, I am happy,
I won't let you appropriate it.
So yeah, people love me.
And I'll never face you by myself again.
So hell no,
You don't own me.

Prompt: What does spirit mean to you? Think of the people, places and things that demand or diminish your queer spirit. This is an opportunity to speak to those spirits that don't fill you up. Let's call them your SPIRIT THIEVES. Write a letter to your spirit thieves letting them know what they've taken from you. State your demands. What do you need from them? Threaten them if necessary, and make ultimatums.

I Sigh

Sometimes, instead of sending desperation into the world by
    force, I sigh.
In many ways, turning it—the speed, the volume—to one is
    what a life needs: a sigh.

For anger, I grab it, slow it with calm thinking and patience,
Sedating the thunderstorm
Whose cracks and pows threaten
A strike to those I love. I sigh.

For sadness, I hold it, I let it happen instead of banishing it.
When I breathe, it seeps through like coffee through a filter.
I have a right to sadness, because I'll keep breathing; I sigh.

For anxiety, I slow down and debunk that marathon of thought.
There's no reason to fear, most of the time.
The butterflies will lay still when I sigh.

So again, I sigh.
We run so far, so fast,
But we often forget one thing to learn.
The world should sigh.

Prompt: Before you write, close your eyes and spend a bit of time listening to your breath. Breathe in through your nose and out of your mouth. What are you taking in as you inhale? What are you releasing as you exhale? Recall a time when an intense emotion (or more than one) overcame you. What was your remedy? Open your toolbox of coping mechanisms. How do you deal?

EVAN ANCON CAZALAS

(he/they)

Memphis, TN

Rhythm of Memphis

The rhythm of my heart aches for Memphis to be great.

A place Tennessee lawmakers hate.

Tennessee don't care about Memphis or me.

Tennessee wants Memphis to leave.

Have you sat in that house of lies?

The rhythm of Memphis ain't seen in those hallways of law.

A ping pong from my representatives to the ones in Fayette County.

They sit in their majority and Memphis' voice is sworn to not be heard.

Shelby County votes are always trumped by ignorance.

HIV rates are on the rise and the governor cuts ties.

Lawmakers smile and say "abstinence is the key

so HIV is something that we shouldn't see."

Memphis still skyrockets with these new cases that shouldn't be.

Tennessee removes funds and Memphis

has to learn to beat on without this huge support.

The target is trans kids these days.

In that house of lies they listen to mother after
mother say how without trans health care
their child would not be here today.
They listen to teens as they tell their story.
They listen to doctors.
But they do not hear us,
too buried in their biases that want to squash our queer hearts
    to care.
On Saturday, in Memphis, I sit with trans kids like me.
Together we create a rhythm that is consistent and safe.
On Monday, I sit in a place that doesn't care about them or me.
A place where the rhythm is ruthless and cold.
My life will always tell me to write.
I have been too quiet, and I can't anymore.
My writing and voice will help Memphis push forward.
Too many years of being quiet and I burst.
My heart belongs to my city, my home, Memphis, Tennessee.

Prompt: As queer people, we have unique relationships to the place we live.
Write an ode to your hometown, the place you currently reside, or to a
city you dream of visiting someday. What does it provide you with? What
does it refuse to give?

ERIC EUBANK

(they/them)

Montrose, CA

To Be Queer Is

To be queer is to feel.

> To feel as though you're playing a game, only you don't
> know how to play it.
>> Where the cards are stacked against you and you're
>> a piece of a puzzle that
>> doesn't quite fit.

To be queer is to fear.

> To fear what will happen if you dare to be,
>> what people will say if you live unbeholden to the
>> body and heart they say you
>> should have,
>>> who will leave you behind because they can't
>>> stand to share a space with
>>> authenticity.

To be queer is to wish.

> To wish it could all go away, that something would change.
>> If not now, then one day.

16

But in queerness, there is so much more.
> In queerness, there is more than feelings of confusion and pain,
>> more than fears of what might happen someday,
>> more than wishing for more.

In queerness lies power.
In queerness lies beauty and joy and connection.
In queerness lies action; a chorus of voices meant to be heard.

In queerness lies feelings of freedom in color, a wash more potent than life itself.
> Fears subsided by light.
> Wishes of telling a single lost spirit or soul that to be queer is simply to feel.

Prompt: Tell the world what being queer means to you. You can use the title of this poem as the prompt, repeating it as many times as you want. Or you can free-form it into being. Just reach down into your most personal experience of being LGBTQIA+.

STELLAN KNOWLES

(he/him/his)

Aurora, CO

True Pride

You say you see me, you cherish me, you just wish
I could be a steady presence in our family,
a hearty carrier of our legacy.
So I try, I show up proud

only for you to cast me away.

In the depths of your attic, I whistle a solemn tune.
My mouth goes dry as my tears collect dust.
I am boxed in, buried
and forgotten.

Summer turns to winter,
I notice the items surrounding me begin to shimmer:
A hot pink sash once placed over the black
-and-silver suit.

The orange t-shirt I wore
to the family reunion—

full of people I'd never met. Connection
and healing at the Black Trans Advocacy Conference.

The yellow bottle of lemon soap I was gifted
for serving as a storyteller
on a sunny Saturday
during Trans Awareness Week.

The green hiking shoes I wore to traverse
the ranch. It was wet and cold
and worth my while, exploring
masculinity in the mountains of Colorado.

Turquoise paintbrushes, used
to compete for a Trans and Disability
Art Show—a flower struggling to stay rooted
and petal-full in the acid rain.

The velvety indigo bag containing
a harmonious relationship
with my body. Before T, I wondered
if I would ever appreciate a mirror.

A violet weighted eye mask which once
smelled heavenly. I began using it
after top surgery, when sleep
wasn't easy.

It still soothes my spirits now,
almost as well as my lovely girlfriend, Violet.

After acknowledging everything in gratitude, I rise to my feet.
Lemon and lavender whirling 'round me,
paintbrushes brandished to clear the musk,
the shirt and sash slip over my head. I lace up my shoes,

the medicine bag glides, as if pulled by its drawstrings—
they wrap my wrist and lead me to the window.
I open it and fly
on the wings of pride.

Prompt: Write a letter to a corporation, a leader, or some kind of entity explaining how they could really be supportive of queer youth (without being performative.) Alternatively, write a piece of prose, poetry, or song about genuine (non-performative) activism.

PARKER MACKENZIE

(she/they)

Clearfield, UT

Fear Not. I'm Practiced

Secrets spill from my protruding lips,
onto the white page of a fragile promise.
Trusting it with my deep well of secrets,
trusting it with my well-hidden longing.

In my chastity—my obsession with "perfection"—
I chased approval instead of happiness:
Come home. Make dinner. Kiss husband.
A taming that could only become my satisfaction.
I listened to the elderly, cranky voices of wisdom.
"This is how you're built. This is what you're suited for.
Eve from Adam's rib, her virgin flower for his great mind,
fit together perfectly—who would ever want more?"
And they warned me of the sinners that would come for
me:
with voices of honey and promises of something greater.
How their eyes would try to hypnotize my body
and whisper to my soul that they had come to save
me.

21

So I sat with reverence in a cavernous chapel
and in the quiet of believing this was all of my desire,
I would paint my nails the color of a newborn's nursery:
an innocent pink nestled in the unkemptness of my hands.
And in my prayers I would repeat: "I am divinity, surely."
And at night, my face would wrinkle horribly—
telling of nightmares that I would bury in the morning
beneath the pretty dresses and makeup palettes and
repeating,
"Pregnancy is a gift from God that makes me divine, surely."
"Becoming a wife is a blessing from God to make me divine,
surely."

"I am divinity, surely." "I am divinity, surely."
Then, dragged into my routine, came a wild song
with a mask of modest human connection.
It seemed like it would only be a moment to wander,
then back to my perfect path of ascension.
And in a fire-like lighting,
in a blaze of wishing stars,
in an echoing symphony of
tense
but lovely
quiet,
her gaze did not break away from mine at all.
She reached inside of my heart
and began to take out
everything that isolated me:

22

the tokophobia hidden in my mascara.
The chains made of wedding rings holding me captive in my
bed sheets.
The wrinkles in my ceiling that drew out my cousin's glossy
eyes
as he shrunk into a realization
that everything he wanted to be
now belonged to a god he had never seen
and the wife
he had just promised eternity.

Then her hands gently took my jaw
and I could no longer remember
what I had wanted,
but I felt her laugh melt into my teeth.
And I wanted her eyes to become my own—
to see everything the way she did,
and she heard my wish.
And before me grew fields of flowers we ran
through in the summer,
plates and plates of cookies we would bake in the winter,
the smell of her sweat and the sound of her voice woven
into her scarf in the fall,
and in spring,
when the rain came to drown my joy
and the storms came to punish me,
she would be there to hold me
and, like a pro-baseball player,

pitch my fears back into the universe,
      straight into wisdom's stupid face.

                    And the sinner came to save me.

Prompt: Give voice to a secret or a story or a belief that feels scary or embarrassing. Allow the passion and intensity of the unlived lives inside of you to be fully expressed. Unleash your Self.

How to Take Care

I used to sleep in an empty room,
void of myself.
Up for school,
straighten my hair
and put on ballet flats.

I used to dream in an empty room.
Find reasons to stay.
Find reasons to try.
Find reasons to exist
and stare at a popcorn ceiling.

I used to be a blank canvas
offering myself to the world.
Sketching from strangers,
finger painting from bullies,
brushstrokes from friends
and judgment from family.

I used to believe in love,
but not the kind with pretty flowers.
Not the kind with gentle touch.
Not the kind with calling out from work
and not the kind with joint bank accounts.

Until one day,

a light shone through the window,
painted me in truth, saying,
"alive."
Twirled my curly hair in its fingers,
saying, "Come and see, my dear."
And the stars in my eyes
led me to think that maybe it was right.

Now I sit alone in a place of my own
figuring out myself.
Up for life,
straighten my bangs
and put on combat boots.

Now I dream in a place of my own.
Find the path my own way.
Find the reality my own way.
Find authenticity my own way
and stare at the posters on my ceiling.

Now I am a closed-off exhibit
only a select few may enter.
Do not touch me when I say no.
Do not laugh at me when I am myself.
Do not betray me or use me for money
and believe me when I say that I bite back.

I still believe in love,

but not the kind with pretty flowers.
Not the kind with gentle touch.
Not the kind with calling out from work
and not the kind with joint bank accounts.

Yes, I still believe in love,
but it's the kind that everyone fears.
The kind that people run away from.
The kind that doesn't require anyone else
and the kind that treats me well.

Prompt: How is the life you lead today different from the one you dreamed up for yourself when you were young? How has queerness influenced your vision of your perfect future?

I watch girls build houses

I watch girls build houses.
Not of clay, nor straw,
but of smiling.
Talking about her favorite things,
with a glistening in her eyes,
and it makes the world go around.

I watch girls build houses.
Not of stone, nor brick,
but of recipes.
Drop baggage, shoes off,
stretch out on the couch
while she boils a pot of love.

I watch girls build houses.
Not of wood, nor cement,
but of trying
to step in time
with the beat of the music
instead of the anxiety of the mind.

I watch girls build houses.
Not of drywall, nor plywood,
but of free tampons and toiletries.
Sitting in circles on the floor;

"Toxic shock syndrome?!"
"Nope. Not in a million years."

I watch girls build houses.
Not of tissue paper, nor ribbons,
but of giving.
"I'm sorry," "I'm sorry," "I'm sorry."
What else can I say?
"I'm sorry," "I'm sorry," "I'm sorry."

I watch girls build houses.
Not of bracelet charms, nor hair ties,
but of holding hands.
Understanding how and why
you don't want to talk.
You just want to cry.

I watch girls build houses.
Not of special creams, nor mirror shards,
but of example.
Scold every surprise wrinkle,
and I have decided
that I will do the opposite.

I watch girls build houses.
Not of trampolines, nor dollhouses,
but of secrets.

Now that I'm older,
I understand why they always felt
like a sacred oath.

I watch girls build houses.
Not of fragile altars, nor prayer beads,
but of sacrifice.
The paintings of Mary;
first holding God's Savior,
then holding her dead son.

I watch girls build houses.
Not of ice cream, nor heating pads,
but of emotions.
Men shame and degrade,
but they still come to us
to feel human.

I watch girls build houses.
Not of picking fingernails, nor hiding in closets,
but of screaming.
Writing out as adults
how their childhoods were stolen,
then reclaiming them,
but it doesn't quite fit where it once did.

I watch girls build houses.
Not of prison bars, nor court hearings,

but of days.
Sitting in loneliness,
or unhinged chaos,
always waiting for something.

I watch girls build houses.
Not of vanilla ice cream, nor full length skirts,
but of power.
Posing in windows lined with neon red lighting,
and her subtle movements beckon men
to pay for every time they called a woman, "Slut".

I watch girls build houses.
Not of pretty dresses, nor pretzel bags,
but of courage.
Walking into the first day of kindergarten
or an abortion clinic down the road,
and finding ways to make the best of something scary.

I watch girls build houses.
Not of hospital gowns, nor shallow breathing,
but of persistence.
Exhausted physically and mentally
giving birth on the second floor,
or receiving treatment on the fourth.

I watch girls build houses.
Not of big muscles, nor wall-leaning,

but of staring.
Hearing them describe
the colors of eyes
like melting into a handmade quilt.

I watch girls build houses.
Not of hard hats, nor paint rollers,
but of imagination.
Let's paint the ceiling with clouds!
Or stars!
And ignore everyone who says it's childish.

I watch girls build houses.
Not of ten inch heels, nor sparkly eyeshadow,
but of strength.
Go out into the world
wearing bright pink to the grocery store,
and telling perverts to "Fuck off!"

I watch girls build houses.
Not of gavels, nor thick folders,
but of persistence.
No matter what the law says,
in this patriarchy
it is and will always be
my body.

I watch girls build houses.

And everyone rolls their eyes,
like they already know that.
Cause we've all seen a woman
get up in the morning
and hold her head in her hands
every day
for decades.

But I wish they could see
what I see—
what I've watched women do.

I've watched them build houses,
till I fall asleep
dreaming of how, I'll build one too.

Prompt: Intuition is the ability to understand something immediately, without the need for conscious reasoning. We could say that queer people have a slightly more developed sense of intuition because so much of who we are is developed without the need for conscious reasoning. Our bodies and hearts tell us what's what. Write a poem about something or someone that you know intuitively.

what my car keys speak of me

What does time see
through the eyes of vicious beasts?
To figure out how to exist...
by your own admission— your permission.
You go on your own way.
A lonely, but free road to drive along.
You can sleep with all your stuffed animals
and no one tells you to grow up their way.

What does time see
through the eyes of unspeakable things?
To figure out how to look up,
by your own willpower— your decision.
You go on your own way.
A sometimes tragic, but fulfilling road to swerve along.
You can scream rap on the drive home:
"I'll get through it my own way!
I'll get through it my own way."

And somehow you always do.
Even when people laugh in your face
about the way you talk or dress.
Even when you feel unhappy
and everyone else pretends they are.
Even when the day is over
and your body aches immensely,

and the weight of petty remarks
drags your shoulders down...
you still make sure to have your tea
every night before bed,
pet your cats and clean their fountain,
and work on the things you love
because the world could never stop you
from chasing your own kind of happiness.

And you'll find it one day.
That's inevitable.

Prompt: "Queer and trans people, especially youth, are in a historical moment when it's not easy to trust being witnessed, perceived. Will it be safe? How will important parts of ourselves be remembered or punished? It takes practice and assurance to know that it is possible to just be. Here, we consider the objects around us who may experience us neutrally, lovingly, and in life's quiet moments where we often feel most human."

—Lexie Bean

BLUEBIRD MONROE

(he/him)

North Charleston, SC

music brain

the beat is in my bone
the jump is in my blood
i feel as my chest beats and bumps
the rhythmic way my heart pumps
my mind thumps through the sound
the reason i live through it all
the reason i write it all down
scribbled on papers scattered around
for when i can't cry out
swing with the song
sing with the sound
they ring in my ear
they sing what i've said
they live in my bed
right where i lay my head
music is the reason my life's everlasting
the music in my mind
to the music out my mouth
my soul is dedicated to the rhythm and sway of a tune

any tune my heart can play
its bumps with the beat of a triplet quarter
the rhythm of the beat runs the world that i strive for
i had never lived 'til the notes blew through my breath
they consume my whole being and body
life is a riddle
music is the answer
no longer alone because i have the rhythm to guide me through
the rhyme

Prompt: Listen close. Can you hear it? What is the heartbeat of your creative rhythm? Underneath all of the noise and music, what's there, as reliable as your pulse? Maybe you want to explore the rhythm of your words to express something only you know about yourself. Score your inner life.

LILY ARIEL MUELLER

(they/she/he)

Webster, MA

APARTMENT 111

With thanks to Matthew Burgess.

                  someday,
you will cut your own hair,

                                  cut them off.

someone bold-
faced sits on the sink, watching
feathers fall to the bathroom floor.
they adjust your hands, now and then.
move to their own music.
pick at the odd ends.

                            neighbors hear you laughing.
you get a headache from the smell of dye
and lay down, blue fingertips
smiling.

your roommate smokes
and you watch the fire flickering
with their breath through the screen door.

38

it doesn't bother you
until   their cough brings their laughter,
                                    everything,

                                                to a stop.

it scares you. always will.
their disregard for their days.
you don't want to imagine a world without them in it.

still,
you pause the movie,
make tea with honey,
sit beside them in the cool air
just a moment.

they play music late into the night,
never take out the trash,
wear your favorite shirt without asking.
they hate the cats.

                            but you remember
                              your togethers:
                doctor's appointments, job interviews,
                          trips back to the town
                you never felt at home in, all the days
                          determined to derail you.

                          you remember yourself,
                          your propensity to forget
                        everything angry and contrary

you cannot contain.

and you remember
that you love these things. here
is the family
you've been looking for
all this time. here
is the blood.
someday, there will be dancing.

sunlight   *rooftop*

                midnight   *barefoot*

you will remember the feeling
of untouchability.
infinite.

remember
you are forever coming of age.

someday, it will be sunday.
you will be
in love
and making breakfast, shoulder to shoulder, happy
smells of burnt butter,
sticky maple fingers.
you will use the paper dishes—you won't even mind.
in this tiny kitchen, this new home,

every day is a day of rest.

sit down, sweetheart.
stop a while.
nothing's coming to get you.

Prompt: For some queer people, the biological family can be a complicated situation, and when that is the case, the writer Armistead Maupin suggests that we begin looking for our logical family. Write a poem or a song or letter describing your logical family. Who are they? How do they make you feel? This can be based on a real experience or a hope for the future.

Dearest

With thanks to Cherie Rowe.

hush, stop fussing,
busy those buckling fingers,
hold them above your heart.

stop prying at old wounds,
those handprints
of whitened tissue.

there's nothing to find there, love.

all that time,
the soil, your roots,
the seasons and
all that poison
was not your fault.

                     but this is.

   so   Stop.
   so   Breathe.

                                   so
              press your forehead to the passenger window
                  and grow dizzy with the passing leaves.

lose count of yellow lines,
cross-eyed,
drifting.

These are the answers you're looking for.

so
curl your knees to your chest
until the years peel back
and spin
like sunlight against the shadows
of the crooked house
you once called home,
like the dancer
you dreamed of becoming.

Here are the answers you're looking for.

so
eyes up.
the earth will wait for you.

reach your palms
into infinity, try to touch
the sky, its stars,
the cool breeze
of the next season.

flinch at the rain
and smile.

think about god
and kindergarten.

wake up
with wings

like those of the hummingbird
you once buried.

Finally, the answers
you've been looking for.

Prompt: Write a letter or a poem addressed to your younger self. What are some things you wish you knew when you were five, seven, ten, twelve or thirteen? What can you tell your younger self about your queer life right now that they might need to know?

sit on the floor

come through the windows.
laugh. cry.

                        this is your space.

i am a first name,
here to calm the storms.

learn what you will.
take what you need.

you are who you are,
and you'll be who you'll be.
the night sky shifts,
and you might too—

                        may your phases be beautiful,
                        and beautifully remembered.
in this life, it's all about kindness.
about care. the oldest take in the book, but
my friends,
love each other.

let us be a beacon.

the truth is
you may never know

who you are. you are anything
other than stagnant,
definable, explicable.
but let's enjoy trying to find out
together.

it will be an honor to meet you
each and every day.

                this place will be
                a home

for everyone yet-to-come,
for every bygone soul.
i care who you are.
i care so much.

tell me everything,
and we will change
for the better.

Prompt: What is your Queericulum (queer curriculum)? What's the subject that you are teaching, and what's the title of your class? Any special instructions for your students? Make it your ideal back-to-school experience.

Still Here

With thanks to Sparrow Murray

question: should life be bearable? is it?
hypothesis: i take ten pills,
more, every day, to stop me from
goodbyes. i used to feel like my brain
was boiling. like my hands weren't mine.
i didn't trust anyone, myself. i wonder if
my love is all just chemical.
i don't know what would've happened to me
in another time. see, i am not brave—
i would have married men and bore children,
left the world small and unfinished. i am sorry
i need help to exist, to be
kind. thank you for waiting.
maybe the next life will be gentler.

Prompt: The sonnet is a fourteen-line poem written in iambic pentameter, employing one of several rhyme schemes, and adhering to a tightly structured thematic organization. What if you queered the form? Forget the rhyme scheme, maybe it's more than fourteen lines, and who says it has to be in iambic pentameter? Make it your own and write about what it feels like to be you, a queer person in the 21st century.

ARI OCHOA PETZOLD

(they/them)
Puebla, MX

Corazón de Pollo

Remember when you left math class in tears and your
Dad said
you feel things so deeply because
you got a chicken's heart?

Chicken Heart,
Gender is not a requisite for love. Your heart
has been held by tender, clean,
strong, and calloused hands.

Chicken Heart,
You
know yourself so deeply that strangers' faces
wrinkle with a smile as you pass by.

Chicken Heart,
You don't treat friendship differently than romance
and that has put you in trouble. Stay careful
not to drop either.

Chicken Heart,

> I think you love like your grandfather, with all the protocol
> and gentlemanliness. You aren't allowed to touch before
> two heart-wrenching conversations. A handful of poems.

Chicken Heart,

> You are kept in a wooden box with golden rimming.
> Guarded in the chaos of passion, only let out around
> the steadiness of companionship.

Corazòn de Pollo,

> It does not mean coward, but rather softness.

*Prompt: Write step by step directions to a favorite place—feel free to create
a map to accompany your writing if useful. What do you carry with you?
Who and what passes your body on the way there? Who and what sees you
on the way there? This can be an imagined or real place, past, present or
future.*

Knowledge

With thanks to Genaro Medina Ramos

O nic yac ipan Cuauhtlahtli ihuihpa ni tlazaloz itech cemana-
huac.

Ni tlahtlania Ozomatli
–¿Quenin nehnemi ipan cuahme?
Ni tlahtlania Cuauhtli
–¿Quenin platani itech ihuicatl?
Ni tlahtlania Michin
–Quenin matema ipan ailhuicatl?

Ihcuac o nic tlahtlaniaya Miztli
quenin mo oliniya. Yehuatl o nech nanquiliz:
–¿Tlen ti chihuaz ican nin tlamachiliztli?
O nic ili –Nic hualmocuepaz ipan noaltepetl
Huan ni tlazaloz quenin ce nemi ican nelmelahualiztli.

Zatepan Miztli o nech tlahtlani –¿Tlen tinech maxtiz nehuatl?
O nic ili –¿Tlen cualtiz nimitz machtiz?
Miztli o nech nanquili:

–Quenin Ozomatli nehnemi ipan cuahme
Quenin Cuauhtli platani ipan ilhuicatl
Quenin Michin matema ipan alhuicatl
Quenin Miztli mo oliniya, huan

Quenin Tlacame huan Cihuame o qui ixhuitiquen
tlahtolli ihuihpa moahzicamatiz itech nochin cemanahuac.

I went out into the forest to learn how plants make
food, how bacteria de-constructs, how fungi grow from death.

I asked for the monkey to teach me how to travel through
the trees,
I asked the hawk to teach me how to soar
the skies.
I asked the fish to teach me how to roam
the rivers.

Then, I asked the cat for the knowledge of balance.
She asked, "What are you going to do with all this knowledge?"
I said, I will go back to my village, and learn, learn and learn
how to wield it right.
She asked, "And what are you going to teach me?"
"What do I have to teach you?" I asked.

The balance of the cat,
the way a fish roams the river, a hawk soars
through the sky, a monkey travels
the trees, the fungi grow through death,
plants make food and bacteria deconstructs.

How humans create language to understand it all.

Wet Soup

Wet soup.
My grandmother teaches me how to make soup,
and I thank her for the heat,
The equilibrium of ingredients and spices
that go overboard by her hand when she adds too much salt.

Wet soup.
There's comfort in repeating things twice:
Sopa mojada, chai tea, Azezenca river.
My grandma cuts deep
into my mother, and she cuts
into myself, and I, well, take the knife
and balance it carefully between my tips.

When you know how to cook,
you are ready to hook up into marriage.
Give away your life for the state, for a union
that will cut and cut and cut until
someone stops repeating. We say things twice,
I gather, to make sure people from two different places
understand that what they are eating is soup,
and it is indeed a food that is wet.

That way you do not mistake the ability to choose who to
    marry,
with the ability to choose to marry.

My grandmother teaches me how to make soup,
repeats the steps once, twice, until I have put more than
    enough salt,
until, like her, I know how to wield a knife.

Prompt: The writer Mark Matousek wrote, "We learn the world from our mother's face." But it could also be said that we learn a lot from our grandparents, our siblings, our queer ancestors, and from our enemies. Write about a moment in your young life when you learned something from an elder. Was it true? Did you have to go back and revise the lesson learned? Or is it something that will travel with you through time?

SEOYEON PARK

(they/she)
Austin, TX

Enough

With help from August Greenwood.

breathe in, breathe out—
let it go.

let it happen.

oh, *"daughter of cups,*
everything to offer, and it's never enough—"

stop. breathe in.

breathe out. let it go—
it will be enough.

it will be enough.

Prompt: Our bodies are constantly providing us with information about what's happening in the world around us and also within us. Do you trust the information that your body is giving you? Listen deeply to what your body is saying right now and let it speak to you. Or, if you prefer, speak to your body and tell it what you need it to know.

minor second

any two or more notes
played simultaneously
is called a harmony.
i stepped from you
(another note for the family chord)
we play in dissonant harmony
until one of us dies
or until i'm cut from your life,
cast out for crimes against the Father,
whichever comes first.
so i know when to run,
but not how to do it.
how to speak,
but not in your language.
where home is,
but not when i'm honest.
how to love you
through the half step.
because any two or more notes played simultaneously
is still called a harmony.

Prompt: What is something in your life (internal or external) that is not in harmony with your queerness? How can you create harmony between your queerness and that entity?

One Year Ago

i can hold my soul in the palms of my hands, glowing, warm
like rolling water between your fingers.

when my soul light glows
so bright that it burns
(just a little, like texas in june)

i sing.
and the notes spill from my mouth,
tumbling, soaring, floating off into the sky

and before i know it
my soul slips out from my hands
growing wings, growing feathers, growing hollow bones.

once, i gave my soul to another—
wide-eyed, trusting, chirping a tune,
but it grated on her nerves

too constant, too loud, too aggravating.
she tore the wings off of this bird
and told it not to sing,

but that was one year ago.
and soon it will turn into twenty,
and i will have forgotten her name.

i will forget what it's like
to want something bad for me,
or to grieve for someone that is still alive.

i hold my soul in the palms of my hands,
glowing, warm,
burning like texas in june.

Prompt: Consider a hurt that lives in you. Create a poem or a song that can hold that hurt so you don't have to carry it with you anymore. Create a home for the hurt that's worthy of its importance in your life.

You Must

you have to trust you have to trust you have to trust
you have to trust you have to trust you have to trust
you have to trust you have to trust you have to trust
you have to trust you have to trust you have to trust
you have to trust you have to trust you have to trust
you have to trust you have to trust you have to trust
you have to trust you have to trust you have to trust
you have to trust you have to trust you have to trust
you have to trust **you have to you have to you
have to.**

you will eat yourself alive if you don't.

*Prompt: Choose something that repeats in your life and write it down.
Maybe it's just one word, a pattern of behavior, a phrase, or a person,
place, or thing. Then write it again. And again. And again. Write it until
something new occurs to you. Let the repetition take you to the next thing.
Or you can use repetition to inspire a poem using repetition. Be sure to let
the repetition emphasize the FEELING you want to convey, and not just
the thought. Do you need me to repeat the instructions?*

PIP

(they/them)
Philadelphia, PA

Sun and Moon

The sun and moon are on opposite sides of the earth just about
    every day,
much like the opposite sides of me, Pip and Kayla,
my home and my queerness.

At school is when all my stars get to burn. It doesn't matter
how bright I am. No matter the words
there's a part of me that hides on the other side of the world.

But despite that, I can't separate them. I can only make
one night and one day
until one day the solar eclipse occurs.

Until one day both sides create a unique hue in the sky,
no longer on separate sides
but in the middle, sharing that spotlight.

I don't expect everyone to look without their tinted glasses,
those fearing to get infected,

fearing that somehow they will somehow get harmed,

but the ones who will look without any protection will see
my beauty. They'll come with cameras
ready to photograph my core,

and no amount of audacity will separate
my sun and my moon—
one day they will only grow radiant.

*Prompt: Go outside and notice the world around you. Choose one aspect
of the natural world and use it as the inspiration for your writing. What
is that tree trying to tell you? Can you allow the grass to find its way into
your writing? What does the sky have to say about your queerness?*

SAM SILVA

(he/they)

Mexico City, MX

For Her

When I was born, a nurse told my mom I would be a stubborn
    person.
Something about how my hair was beginning to grow
Indicated I would have a strong character.
I wish I could find that nurse. Ask her how she realized.

I remember being four years old on the school playground,
Accidentally learning about the binary for the first time.
Before that, my parents had learned the nurse was right,
My hair had sealed my unruly behavior—
But there I was, some classmates screaming at me to be a girl.

I was nine years old when I got my first death threat.
It was accompanied by two broken ribs.
My voice was also stolen that day. I was told it was my fault.
If I was normal, stuck to what was expected from me,
nothing would have happened.
They didn't know I can't do that.

I found a photo, probably two weeks after that.
I was showing my new Chewbacca mask.
I didn't understand why I couldn't go to school.
I was just happy with my mask.

I spent nights completely lost,
Taking notes of all the flaws I wished I could make disappear.
I created a new mask—one made out of tears and fear;
One made out of death threats and broken bones;
A mask that took me years to take off.

A mask that fell with the soft hum of strands
And tears of joy falling to the ground.
For the first time, I saw my hair grow back from the start.
Saw the reminder of the kid I was—the one who ran around
Without understanding what awaited her.

I write for her, who I couldn't protect.

Prompt: The poet Joe Brainard created an epic poem entitled, "I Remember." An "I Remember" poem can be simply a list of memories, but it can also be a collection of memories that reveals something about yourself to yourself or a spell invoking a particular atmosphere or truth.

Grandfather

When I was five years old, my grandfather "teached" me how
    to balance
A TV controller on my finger.

He helped me catch it in case it fell.
To this day when I'm watching TV, I find myself balancing
The pieces from side to side.

I can still feel his presence in his jacket, even after so many washes.
The scent of cigarettes and old cologne accompanies me.
He always had it zipped up.
I broke the zipper a few weeks ago.

Whenever I came home crying, feeling lost, he would comfort
    me.
We would watch TV, balancing the controller.

I carry a necklace. He wore it as a symbol of devotion
To La Virgen de Guadalupe and my grandma.
I wear it as a reminder of his being.

I say 'thank you' instead of 'bless you.'
I call grapes *onions with sugar.*
I'm like him.

I was his favorite, favorite grandkid.

I was his first and only granddaughter.
One of our last conversations,
he held my hands and came to a realization
that took me so much time.
It took me years.

You're not my granddaughter, you're my grandson, but you're
    still my favorite.

Prompt: How does balance relate to your writing? To your queerness?
Write a poem, a list, a letter, a story, that includes the element of balance.
Go literal or make it poetic. Use balance as your muse!

LILY THOMAS

(she/her)

San Antonio, TX

on jealousy

It's greed, it's need, it's pain and hunger pangs.
It's angry, wretched, loud and stifling.
It's suffocating, scornful—

I shouldn't say this, yes, I know it's wrong
but what else can I do save sing my song
and mourn for everything I should have done?

My thoughts engulf me in these flames, too bright
they burn like passion through the night
and scar my skin, so raw and broken.

I'm sorry, I confess this to you here.
I could ignore it until it sears,
twist it into a fight. It's unbecoming, lust;
my craven urge, my emerald eyes.

Prompt: Describe a feeling from the inside out. By writing about your particular relationship to that feeling, the universal is revealed. Write about how your body responds to the feeling. Where does it live in your body when you're NOT feeling it? When the feeling passes, what has it taught you?

summertime in texas

In the summer, only a few weeks ago
at the Guadalupe River, thirty minutes from my home,
we threw rocks out into the water
and the fish tickled our toes.
Today it was raining, pouring down onto me
as I got my passport renewed—I ran
out the doors and into the parking lot
and when I got in the car I was drenched.
Summer is humid this year,
as it always is in South Texas.
It's hot, but the rain cools us down
and we float down the river.
I always ask myself, why do I still live here?
I never liked Texas—my home,
my family, my life.
Even when the cicadas roar
and sun sears my skin—
it's home. Airplanes soar
overhead. I mean to say, it's beautiful
if you look from outside.
I hope I can stay and escape.
The ringing in my ears
is constant. My A/C is off.
I turn on a fan, an air purifier,
and turn out the lights
to sleep.

Prompt: THE NINE STEP POEM

　1. Describe the last time you were submerged in a body of water.

　2. Describe something that you observed this week, or something right in front of you.

　3. Start a sentence with, "Summer is..."

　4. Ask a question.

　5. Describe something you can see right now.

　6. Start a sentence with, "What I mean to say is..."

　7. Start a sentence with, "I wish" or "I hope."

　8. Describe something you can hear right now.

　9. Write something about what happens right before you fall asleep.

P.S. Feel free to leave out, rearrange, or add to any of the steps. Make it your own.

—Sparrow Murray

SIMON VENTURA

(he/him)

Las Vegas, NV

From Here I Build

In philosophy, we talk a lot about how we know
what we know is true. We are introduced
to the idea of an Archimedean point—one place
in the face of uncertainty where we see clearly—
and from there we build.

My experience with gender and myself was uncertain,
at first. Instead of being given the tools and community
and language I needed, I was told that I was crazy
and what I was feeling wasn't real. I didn't have anything
certain in the beginning. I had to start from scratch
all on my own. I needed to build
my own Archimedean point.

I started as small as I could,
as small as I needed to:
I feel better in jeans than a skirt.
I like my hair short better than long.
Rather than adorned with makeup,

I like my face bare. And from here I've built.

I like it when I'm not put in the girls team
in class competitions. I like it
when people call me
"he". And from here I've built.

Gender is not the binary that I've been told.
There are other people who feel like this.
There is a word for who I am—

I am a boy.
I am transgender.
I am Simon.

       —and from here I will build.

*Prompt: What does it feel like to have someone define you or your queer-
ness as being wrong? What happens to you when someone (other than
yourself) questions your thinking? What is one thing that you know for
sure about yourself, something no one can change your mind about?*

THE WRITERS

Veronica (Vivi) Butler (she/her)
Vivi joined the Future Perfect Project during quarantine to find community and hopes to continue advocating for LGBTQ+ youth as she pursues the next chapter.

Virgil Beaty (they/them)
Born and raised in Philadelphia, PA, Virgil is a creative, always improving their craft. They write, draw and act, all the while finding beauty in the mundane.

Helix Carpenter (it/they/she)
Helix is an aspiring writer who loves to spread their stories of drama, tragedy, and success around the world - with a key sprinkle of thought.

Evan Ancon Cazalas (he/they)
Evan is a transgender teenager navigating growing up in the south who enjoys writing, art, baking, and public speaking.

Eric Eubank (they/them)

Eric is a non-binary writer, student, and storyteller; as both a chronic overthinker and curious soul, they are currently on a journey to find beauty and joy in the everyday.

Stellan Knowles (he/him/his)

Originally from Memphis, TN, Stellan is a multi-talented creative writer, actor, and producer with a passion for storytelling in all its forms.

Parker Mackenzie (she/they)

Parker is a genderfluid, lesbian, multitalented songwriter/singer and your favorite artist's favorite artist's mortuary assistant.

Bluebird Monroe (he/him)

Originally from Charleston, SC, Bluebird is a young artist and activist, and spends his free time being the lead singer of his rock band, acting in musicals, and fighting for trans rights.

Lily Ariel Mueller (they/she/he)

Lily is a New England based curious creative working at the intersections of queerness, disability, memory, imagination, and healing.

Ari Ochoa Petzold (they/them)

Ari is a writer in process that likes dancing to old music and history. One of their goals in mind is to bring to the world stories about the human condition told through the intersectionality of being queer and latine.

Seoyeon Park (they/she)

Seoyeon is a college student studying music and literature, subjects that influence and intertwine with their writing.

Pip (they/them)

Pip! Pip! Cheerio from Philadelphia, PA.

Sam Silva (he/they)

Sam AKA Paradox is a Mexican, transmasc, aspiring drag artist and writer, who also enjoys playing the bass.

Lily Thomas (she/her)

Born and raised in San Antonio, TX, Lily is passionate about the creative arts, having won multiple awards in photography and been recognized for her creative writing and art.

Simon Ventura (he/him)

Simon is an aro/ace trans man aspiring to be a librarian.

SPACE AGREEMENTS

by Emma Jayne Seslowsky,
Program Director

At The Future Perfect Project, we believe queer youth are living in a future that has not yet arrived. In other words, they have quite a lot to teach us about where our world is headed. In our experience, the most successful workshop facilitators don't aim to teach, but rather, to create a safer space for the queer youth to explore their creativity without judgement. Here are some of the ways we aim to keep our participants feeling supported enough to approach the vulnerable act of creating and sharing their original work.

You can remember these space agreements with the acronym **BRICKS**:

- **Be**: Be yourself, be present, be brave, be on time. Remember, everyone in the room has made a commitment to sharing themselves through discussion and writing. All feelings are welcome!

- **R**espect: This can look like using the correct names and pronouns of everyone in the room, not writing about other participants in your work, leaving drama and inside jokes at the door, providing content warnings before sharing about sensitive topics, and actively listening.

- **I** (Speak from the I): Instead of responding to writing with statements about how "everybody" feels, make your responses personal to you: *"I felt really at ease when you read your piece."*

- **C**onfidentiality aka The Vegas Rule: Everything said here stays here. Keep it confidential. However, writers are encouraged to continue working on their pieces outside of the workshop.

- **K**indness: Assume best intentions from everybody in the space. If you hurt someone, tend to the impact: Apologize, take ownership, and move on. If you feel hurt, ask the facilitator to support you in finding a private time to make your pain known, and be open to an apology.

- **S**pace (Make Space, Take Space): If you're someone who shares a lot, you might want to make space for those who don't. And if you're someone who tends to hang back, you might want to be brave and speak more! Remember, every participant will get a chance to share and be heard.

THE WRITING PROMPTS

by Celeste Lecesne, Artistic Director

The best piece of writing advice I ever heard was something that the writer, Grace Paley, often said to her students:

"Write from what you know, but write into what you don't know."

These prompts are not meant to replace what you know about yourself or the world around you; they are here to spark your writing practice and to inspire you to begin writing from what you know. Feel free to use them in whatever way feels right for you. Let them take you to unexpected places, allow yourself to be surprised by whatever feelings or ideas they inspire, free yourself from the pressure of being productive, and just write for the fun of it. Be curious.

The good news is there's no wrong way to approach a writing prompt. What matters is developing a writing practice that is so alive that eventually your words speak not only for you, but also to you.

You'll find some lined pages at the back of this book. Our hope is that you will fill them with what you don't know, and in the process, surprise yourself with who you are becoming.

———

Prompt: Shapeshifting is a special talent that queer people have. We often find ourselves blending into the background to survive, toning down our is-ness to pass, or flaming as a signal that we are unafraid. We can learn a lot about adaptation from our non-human siblings. Transform yourself into an animal, an insect, a flower, a tree or a bird and tell us what you know about the world.

———

Prompt: Every one of us, at every age, is a work in progress. We are never done with the business of liberating ourselves from false notions, old habits and limiting ideas. Make a demand or write a poem, letter, or song to the part of you that is not yet free.

———

Prompt: Do you believe your identity is forever locked into place, or is it something more complicated and fluid? Write about the way you express yourself as a queer person, whether that expression stays the same or transforms from moment to moment. Does your queerness change in relation to the world around you? As the poet ALOK once said, "Look at the seasons darling...Look at the sun, darling, everything else is moving but you. So am I the issue or is your stagnancy the issue?"

Prompt: Can you think of an example from your life when maybe you didn't have the words to describe something that was happening to you? Like a crush, or maybe something about your gender or sexuality— something you intuited about your queer self before you knew what to call it? Tune into YOUR dark place of possibility and listen closely for a prophecy of a possible future, either for yourself or for the world. Abandon conscious reasoning. What do you know?

———

Prompt: What does spirit mean to you? Think of the people, places and things that demand or diminish your queer spirit. This is an opportunity to speak to those spirits that don't fill you up. Let's call them your SPIRIT THIEVES. Write a letter to your spirit thieves letting them know what they've taken from you. State your demands. What do you need from them? Threaten them if necessary, and make ultimatums.

———

Prompt: Before you write, close your eyes and spend a bit of time listening to your breath. Breathe in through your nose and out of your mouth. What are you taking in as you inhale? What are you releasing as you exhale? Recall a time when an intense emotion (or more than one) overcame you. What was your remedy? Open your toolbox of coping mechanisms. How do you deal?

———

Prompt: As queer people, we have unique relationships to the place we live. Write an ode to your hometown, the place you currently reside, or to a city you dream of visiting someday. What does it provide you with? What does it refuse to give?

———

Prompt: Tell the world what being queer means to you. You can use the title of this poem ("To Be Queer Is") as the prompt, repeating it as many times as you want. Or you can free-form it into being. Just reach down into your most personal experience of being LGBTQIA+.

———

Prompt: Write a letter to a corporation, a leader, or some kind of entity explaining how they could really be supportive of queer youth (without being performative). Alternatively, write a piece of prose, poetry, or song about genuine (non-performative) activism.

———

Prompt: Give voice to a secret or a story or a belief that feels scary or embarrassing. Allow the passion and intensity of the unlived lives inside of you to be fully expressed. Unleash your Self.

———

Prompt: How is the life you lead today different from the one you dreamed up for yourself when you were young? How has queerness influenced your vision of your perfect future?

———

Prompt: Intuition is the ability to understand something immediately, without the need for conscious reasoning. We could say that queer people have a slightly more developed sense of intuition because so much of who we are is developed without the need for conscious reasoning. Our bodies and hearts tell us what's what. Write a poem about something or someone that you know intuitively.

———

Prompt: "Queer and trans people, especially youth, are in a historical moment when it's not easy to trust being witnessed, perceived. Will it be safe? How will important parts of ourselves be remembered or punished? It takes practice and assurance to know that it is possible to just be. Here, we consider the objects around us who may experience us neutrally, lovingly, and in life's quiet moments where we often feel most human."

—Lexie Bean

———

Prompt: Listen close. Can you hear it? What is the heartbeat of your creative rhythm? Underneath all of the noise and music, what's there, as reliable as your pulse? Maybe you want to explore the rhythm of your words to express something only you know about yourself. Score your inner life.

———

Prompt: For some queer people, the biological family can be a complicated situation, and when that is the case, the writer Armistead Maupin suggests that we begin looking for our logical family. Write a poem or a song or letter describing your logical family. Who are they? How do they make you feel? This can be based on a real experience or a hope for the future.

Prompt: Write a letter or a poem addressed to your younger self. What are some things you wish you knew when you were five, seven, ten, twelve or thirteen? What can you tell your younger self about your queer life right now that they might need to know?

————

Prompt: What is your Queericulum (queer curriculum)? What's the subject that you are teaching, and what's the title of your class? Any special instructions for your students? Make it your ideal back-to-school experience.

————

Prompt: The sonnet is a fourteen-line poem written in iambic pentameter, employing one of several rhyme schemes, and adhering to a tightly structured thematic organization. What if you queered the form? Forget the rhyme scheme, maybe it's more than fourteen lines, and who says it has to be in iambic pentameter? Make it your own and write about what it feels like to be you, a queer person in the 21st century.

————

Prompt: Write step by step directions to a favorite place—feel free to create a map to accompany your writing if useful. What do you carry with you? Who and what passes your body on the way there? Who and what sees you on the way there? This can be an imagined or real place, past, present or future.

————

Prompt: Queerness can be a constant state of becoming and discovery. When was the last time you allowed yourself to be curious? Write about *it in the style of a folktale. You are encouraged to incorporate fantastical elements, dialogue, and a cast of characters.*

———

Prompt: The writer Mark Matousek wrote, "We learn the world from our mother's face." But it could also be said that we learn a lot from our grandparents, our siblings, our queer ancestors, and from our enemies. Write about a moment in your young life when you learned something from an elder. Was it true? Did you have to go back and revise the lesson learned? Or is it something that will travel with you through time?

———

Prompt: Our bodies are constantly providing us with information about what's happening in the world around us and also within us. Do you trust the information that your body is giving you? Listen deeply to what your body is saying right now and let it speak to you. Or if you prefer, speak to your body and tell it what you need it to know.

———

Prompt: What is something in your life (internal or external) that is not in harmony with your queerness? How can you create harmony between your queerness and that entity?

———

Prompt: Consider a hurt that lives in you. Create a poem or a song that can hold that hurt so you don't have to carry it with you anymore. Create a home for the hurt that's worthy of its importance in your life.

Prompt: Choose something that repeats in your life and write it down. Maybe it's just one word, a pattern of behavior, a phrase, or a person, place, or thing. Then write it again. And again. And again. Write it until something new occurs to you. Let the repetition take you to the next thing. Or you can use repetition to inspire a poem using repetition. Be sure to let the repetition emphasize the FEELING you want to convey, and not just the thought. Do you need me to repeat the instructions?

———

Prompt: Go outside and notice the world around you. Choose one aspect of the natural world and use it as the inspiration for your writing. What is that tree trying to tell you? Can you allow the grass to find its way into your writing? What does the sky have to say about your queerness?

———

Prompt: The poet Joe Brainard created an epic poem entitled, "I Remember." An "I Remember" poem can be simply a list of memories, but it can also be a collection of memories that reveals something about yourself to yourself or a spell invoking a particular atmosphere or truth.

———

Prompt: How does balance relate to your writing? To your queerness? Write a poem, a list, a letter, a story, that includes the element of balance. Go literal or make it poetic. Use balance as your muse!

———

Prompt: Describe a feeling from the inside out. By writing about your particular relationship to that feeling, the universal is revealed. Write about how your body responds to the feeling. Where does it live in your body when you're NOT feeling it? When the feeling passes, what has it taught you?

————

Prompt: THE NINE STEP POEM
1. Describe the last time you were submerged in a body of water.
2. Describe something that you observed this week, or something right in front of you.
3. Start a sentence with, "Summer is..."
4. Ask a question.
5. Describe something you can see right now.
6. Start a sentence with, "What I mean to say is..."
7. Start a sentence with, "I wish" or "I hope."
8. Describe something you can hear right now.
9. Write something about what happens right before you fall asleep.

P.S. Feel free to leave out, rearrange, or add to any of the steps. Make it your own.

—Sparrow Murray

————

Prompt: What does it feel like to have someone define you or your queerness as being wrong? What happens to you when someone (other than yourself) questions your thinking? What is one thing that you know for sure about yourself, something no one can change your mind about?

Write From Your Life

_____

_____

_____

_____

_____

_____

_____

_____

_____

_____

_____

Visit us at thefutureperfectproject.org